THE GIFT OF YOUR WISDOM

USA Today and *The Wall Street Journal* **Best-selling Author**

Alinka Rutkowska

Copyright © 2022 Alinka Rutkowska
Published in the United States by Leaders Press.
www.leaderspress.com

All rights reserved. No part of this book may be reproduced or transmitted in any form or by any means, electronic or mechanical, including photocopying, recording, or by an information storage and retrieval system – except by a reviewer who may quote brief passages in a review to be printed in a magazine or newspaper – without permission in writing from the publisher.

ISBN 978-1-63735-144-4 (pbk)
ISBN 978-1-63735-145-1 (ebook)

Library of Congress Control Number: 2022903214

You are receiving this book because someone we both know said the world would benefit if you shared your wisdom in the form of a book.

We know writing a book can be daunting, but our six-step recipe makes it easier and more fun.

Let's change the world together.

Contents

Can *Your* Book Change the World? 1

Your *Why*..*3*

Introduction to A.U.T.H.O.R. 9

A—Accelerate the Publishing Process 11

U—Uncover Your Outline 15

T—Talk About Your Expertise 35

H—Hack the Writing Phase....................................... 41

O—Optimize the Manuscript.................................... 47

R—Reach Best-Selling Status and Bookstores 51

Now What? 57

Can Your Book Change The World?

Do you remember the last time you read a great book? A book that made a significant impact in your life. A book that became a part of who you are now. Who would you be if you hadn't read that book?

The most inspirational books are written by people just like you and me. Have you ever been inspired to create your own masterpiece? A book to share your wisdom or a book you think can help someone's life? A book that could *change the world*.

Changing the world seems pretty impossible—but what if it isn't?

Your story can inspire others, creating a ripple effect that extends farther than you could ever imagine. Your story can move mountains, move people, and ultimately change the world.

Your Why

Every mission starts with a purpose, a goal, a ***why***.

Before we give you our six-step process to create your masterpiece, let's start with the ***why***. Your ***why*** gives you the energy to pursue the ***how***.

Why should you share your story? Here's why:

1. It gives you **Authority**

    A book establishes you as the expert in your arena, giving you the platform of other thought leaders who have inspired people in similar ways. A popular book can and will make your name synonymous with your industry or area of experience.

2. It grants **Visibility**

    If you are an entrepreneur, coach, speaker, or other service professional, you have a message, service, and/or product to share with your clients. No matter how great and awesome your service or product is, it won't matter if your customers don't know who you are. The key to creating Authority is to reach an audience that needs what you have to offer. Customers, CEOs, and anyone who can benefit from what you have to offer will know who you are once you write a best-selling book.

3. It establishes **Credibility**

    A book is the new calling card for your company. As we said in building your Authority, your book establishes you as an expert. Think of it like this: will you buy an item at a store with no sales, no brand, or no trusted customers?

4. It makes you **Money**

    A properly marketed book is a cash-generating asset. Yes, you can make a profit off of just one book! Imagine selling it to one person? Then 100? Then 1,000? Then 10,000?

5. It opens doors and creates **Invitation**

    Top-ranked books provide many readers with an entrance into your world. We always incorporate a part of us in the books we create. Your customers will know a part of you, and your audience will know who you are, how you are, and what you are.

6. It can build your **Consultancy**

    A best-selling book creates opportunities for speaking engagements and consulting gigs. As an expert, just imagine a group of aviation enthusiasts, global marketers, or microchip engineers willing to pay to learn from you. Mind-blowing!

7. It enshrines your **Legacy**

    Explain to your family and heirs what you did when you were building a business. You get to share your journey—how you overcame obstacles and became who you are now.

Your words will inspire people. People will know you and learn from you.

Now, imagine your book is done.

What has changed in your world and in your readers' worlds?

Just like in those "spot the difference" pictures, look at your life now and picture your life when your book is out.

Example:

Before book: *When prospects, potential partners, or other entrepreneurs ask how best they can get to know me, I almost always dedicate my personal time and do a phone call.*

After book: *When prospects, potential partners, or other entrepreneurs ask how best they can get to know me, I give them a copy of my book first; if we resonate, we continue with a phone call. As a result, I waste much less time and attract only the best fit.*

Spot 5 differences below:

Difference 1/5:

The Gift of Your Wisdom

Difference 2/5:

Difference 3/5:

Difference 4/5:

Difference 5/5:

Notes:

Introduction To A.u.t.h.o.r.

Now that you know why your book needs to be out, let us show you how to make it happen using our proven A.U.T.H.O.R. framework. Our framework has helped 172 authors reach a spot on the *USA Today* and *The Wall Street Journal* best-seller list.

The A.U.T.H.O.R. framework is a process for creating a best-selling book, and you can outsource each step:

A- Accelerate the Publishing Process

U - Uncover Your Outline

T- Talk About Your Expertise

H - Hack the Writing Phase

O - Optimize the Manuscript

R - Reach Best-Selling Status

Ready? Let's get started!

A

Accelerate The Publishing Process

To accelerate the publishing process, you have to understand what the market wants, how your book fits in, and how it stands out.

Why?

I'm sure you've heard stories of authors who spent a decade writing their book only to pitch it to agents and find there is no market need for it!

Here's how we save you years of wasted time.

Accelerating the publishing process is the foundation of book marketing. We find a way to make your book fit in and stand out from the crowd. Once that's done, it allows us to take you through the other steps of the A.U.T.H.O.R. framework in a timely and efficient manner, all the way until your book becomes a best seller.

Let me give you an example. Take our book entitled Outsource Your Book.

First of all, we need to make sure that there is a market for it. When you go to Amazon, you will find several popular categories related to authorship or writing skills. That's great; that means many readers are interested in learning about writing.

The Gift of Your Wisdom

But how do we make sure *Outsource Your Book* stands out? While all the other books talk about the *how*—how to write and how to publish—we talk about the *how not*—how you don't have to do anything and can outsource each step of the way.

That's our unique selling proposition.

Your turn. Let's think about your book.

For this exercise, follow the following steps:

Step 1. Go to Amazon and find three competing titles. Competing titles are books similar to yours and would be on the bookshelf next to yours.

List your three competing titles here:

1.

2.

3.

Now, how does your book stand out?

A Accelerate The Publishing Process

> What makes your book different?
>
>
> Why should readers select your book and not the one next to yours?

Great, now you have your book's Unique Selling Proposition.

U

Uncover Your Outline

The outline is already in your head; it just needs to be uncovered with the help of an experienced professional.

Here's the Ultimate Guide.

BRAIN DUMP

Make a list of the topics you wish to cover in your book; these will roughly map to chapters. We recommend that you do a brain dump of any possible idea you might want to cover. At this point, no idea is a bad idea.

The Gift of Your Wisdom

SHOWCASE

In this section, remove all the really good ideas from the above section that support your main objectives for this particular book.

TABLE OF CONTENTS

To create your table of contents, please look at your showcase ideas. It's important to now arrange these ideas into a logical progression that develops your book idea. It might seem overwhelming, but please don't worry—writing a book is an organic process; it's normal to move topics around as you create it and new conclusions or forgotten elements occur to you. Consider the Table of Contents as a launching pad for your genius.

INTRODUCTION

More details on how to construct your introduction are provided below. It is a good idea to write your introduction last as it often contains an inviting summary of your book's main points meant to captivate your audience. Writing it last will also allow you room to accommodate any changes you make to your book's outline and flow as it develops. Brevity is key—keep your introduction short and to the point so you don't lose your reader.

Tips on how to create a mind-blowing introduction.

Tip 1: START WITH A BANG

Open your book with a bang. It's almost a cliché how important your opening line is, but with the advent of the Internet and so many competing sources of information, it's more important than ever.

Summarize your book concept in one line or paragraph in an attention-grabbing manner.

Tip 2: CLIFFHANGER ANECDOTE

This should be a cliffhanger anecdote that both grabs the reader's attention and establishes your expertise by showing how you would have gotten out of a given situation. (For instance, the CEO of Disney spent eight years building a park in China, and on the day of its launch, two attendees were shot. How would you handle this?)

Tip 3: ESTABLISH YOUR EXPERTISE

Firmly establish your expertise and reputation. Sentences such as, "When I handled a $10 million deal. . ." do an excellent job of framing your expertise in both scale and competence.

Tip 4: MAKE A PROMISE

Make a big promise that will benefit your reader and that your book will deliver; paint a rosy picture of what life with your solution or expertise will look like.

Tip 5: SEGUE TO YOUR FIRST CHAPTER

Now lead your readers directly into your first chapter, e.g., "Now that you know the basics, let's make you an expert."

Note:

We generally find that ten well-developed chapters will give you a book of around 40,000 to 50,000 words. Depending on your needs, it's perfectly fine to have more or fewer chapters.

CHAPTER 1:

Write a one- to two-sentence summary of the chapter and/or include a list of subtopics below.

CHAPTER 2:

Write a one- to two-sentence summary of the chapter and/or include a list of subtopics below.

CHAPTER 3:

Write a one- to two-sentence summary of the chapter and/or include a list of subtopics below.

CHAPTER 4:

Write a one- to two-sentence summary of the chapter and/or include a list of subtopics below.

CHAPTER 5:

Write a one- to two-sentence summary of the chapter and/or include a list of subtopics below.

CHAPTER 6:

Write a one- to two-sentence summary of the chapter and/or include a list of subtopics below.

CHAPTER 7:

Write a one- to two-sentence summary of the chapter and/or include a list of subtopics below.

CHAPTER 8:

Write a one- to two-sentence summary of the chapter and/or include a list of subtopics below.

CHAPTER 9:

Write a one- to two-sentence summary of the chapter and/or include a list of subtopics below.

The Gift of Your Wisdom

CHAPTER 10:

Write a one- to two-sentence summary of the chapter and/or include a list of subtopics below.

Your conclusion will comprise a satisfying ending—a callback to the major points of each chapter, if appropriate—and a call to action so your readers know how to continue their journey now that they've finished your book.

We have left a few blank pages for you to create your own outline.

YOUR BRAIN DUMP GOES HERE

U Uncover Your Outline

Now, let's give it some structure

Use the above "brain dump" to elegantly organize your ideas into well-structured chapters.

CHAPTER 1

CHAPTER 2

CHAPTER 3

CHAPTER 4

CHAPTER 5

CHAPTER 6

CHAPTER 7

CHAPTER 8

CHAPTER 9

U Uncover Your Outline

CHAPTER 10

Talk About Your Expertise

Dennis Andrews spent more than a decade trying to write a corporate memoir of his time at IBM.

Even after spending thousands of dollars on coaches and consultants, he could never write a draft of the book that he dreamed about that did justice to his vision and experiences.

By talking to us and engaging in our fifteen hours of interviews, Dennis was able to finally fulfill that vision with *Too Blue*, his best-selling memoir of the days of the creation of the earliest IBM computers.

Imagine what we can do together!

Here are two ideas to help you:

Idea 1:

Record to your phone and get it transcribed. Paste your transcribed memo here.

T Talk About Your Expertise

Idea 2: Let us help you.

Go to leaderspress.com/chat and book a time to chat about your book idea.

T Talk About Your Expertise

H

Hack The Writing Phase

Even an expert can have a hard time writing a book.

Sometimes the problem is language, sometimes the problem is ability, sometimes the problem is as small as just having enough time.

Regardless of the issue, there's always the danger and fear of putting out a bad book. How do you avoid that? You hack the writing phase. This is the phase where you write your manuscript. If this is your forte, way to go. If not, it's not a problem if you get help.

At Leaders Press, we employ our veteran and expert project managers, writers, and editors to walk you through the process and ensure that you produce the best book possible. We craft your book lovingly by writing the book in your voice!

Check out the Leaders Press website at https://leaderspress.com/ to see how you can get this done in fifteen hours.

Below is where your polished manuscript goes. I know you won't have it right away, but I'm leaving a few blank pages so you can imagine what it will look like when it's done.

The Gift of Your Wisdom

H Hack The Writing Phase

The Gift of Your Wisdom

H Hack The Writing Phase

Optimize The Manuscript

Here is where we start to talk about what I like to call the "heavy lifting." Many don't know how much work goes into publishing a book.

A new author who is doing everything themselves has to consider how they will format their book for both print and e-book. How will they have it edited? When it's published, who will distribute the book to bookstores and online?

All of these processes require a lot of work! In some cases, optimizing your book for distribution can be even more complicated than writing it.

A common mistake for those that go into self-publishing or even the traditional route, is that a new author forges ahead with no idea how to take these steps to produce a book that people will see and want to read.

We bring order to the chaos.

Here are a few blank pages where you can write your ideas on optimizing your manuscript. Please note that this is where you will do the editing, formatting, keywords, categories and your book description for the various retailers. It is important to know the importance of this phase.

The Gift of Your Wisdom

O Optimize The Manuscript

The Gift of Your Wisdom

R

Reach Best-Selling Status And Bookstores

How do you get your book to achieve best-seller status?

Let us show you ***how.***

There are different types of best-seller status—the chief ones are *USA Today*, *The Wall Street Journal,* and Amazon. To hit the *USA Today* and *The Wall Street Journal* lists, and Amazon will take different strategies.

The following is a very condensed strategy I used to launch *Write and Grow Rich*, which became a *USA Today, The Wall* Street Journal, *and Amazon* best seller.

As a consequence of this first successful launch, we've successfully gotten 172 of Leaders Press authors on the *The Wall Street Journal* and *USA Today* best-seller lists.

What if you were to do it yourself?

The first thing to do is find out exactly what is required to hit the *USA Today* best-seller list.

No matter how you're published (traditionally, independently, or via a hybrid publisher), you need to meet the following requirements:

- Sell 6,000 books in a single week. (I had sold 100,000+ books, but you have to sell 6,000 in one week.)
- Only US sales count
- Pre-orders count
- 500+ sales on a retailer other than Amazon
- It must be a paid book
- It can be a solo book or a box set

So how do you sell 6,000 books in a single week?

With the help of co-authors or partners!

If you were to do a launch with 20 authors and you each had a list of 10,000 people, you'd have one giant list of 200,000 (there would be some overlapping but not much). Selling 6,000 books in a week would be much easier with a giant list like that rather than relying on your own list of only tens of thousands.

This is exactly what I did with *Write and Grow Rich*.

The result was that under my leadership, 23 authors and I hit the *USA Today* best-seller list at No. 68 out of 150 books that made the list that week. Now you know how, and because I love you so much, I'm also going to give you two strategies to help you land on the *USA Today* best-seller list.

Running a *USA Today* best-selling press gives me a lot of insight into the world of best sellers, so let's explore launching your book individually versus doing an anthology with other authors.

Become a *USA Today* best seller as a solo author.

To hit the list with an individual book, you need to have a massive following, team up with promotional partners, or run paid ads—ideally all three. To start, consider launching a new release and having a long pre-order period so that your sales accumulate in the months before the launch date.

Also, think realistically about email marketing open and click-through rates. Let's say that 2 percent of your subscribers click to where you send them, and maybe half of the people who land on your book page buy it. To get 6,000 sales, you need 12,000 readers to visit your book's retail page. If 2 percent of your subscribers click, that means you need a list of 600,000 to pull it off.

Do you have a list of 600,000 US-based subscribers (remember, only US sales count)? If you don't, read on.

You might be a long way from a fan base of more than half a million, but others are already there. A leading promotional partner for many authors attempting to hit the list is BookBub, which has millions of readers on its lists.

The challenge with BookBub is that it is very selective; the majority of books submitted are rejected, especially if they are new and without reviews, which is what your pre-order is!

That leaves us with paid traffic. First, you need to figure out where your audience hangs out. To simplify things, let's say it's Facebook. Now, we need to understand what the average cost per click (CPC) is. This number will vary based on the time and your skills. I think it's safe to assume that you can spend between $2 and $5 per click—and that's if you know what you're doing. At a 50 percent book page conversion rate, that means it would cost between $24,000 and $60,000 to attempt to hit the list with ads. And you still have no guarantee of success.

Fortunately, there's a way to increase the odds.

You can work with a pro, such as Leaders Press, that can take you from book ideas all the way to *USA Today* or *The Wall Street Journal* best sellers.

Whether you do it yourself or get professionals to help, you can skyrocket your career, grow your business, and hopefully see your dreams of becoming a best-selling author come true.

So, what's your launch strategy?

Brainstorm it below.

R Reach Best-selling Status And Bookstores

You just went through these exercises because someone we both know said the world would benefit if you shared your wisdom in the form of a book.

There are readers whose lives will change once they read it.

Now What?

If you need help turning your book idea into something great,
let's chat about how we can do this together.

Go to http://leaderspress.com/chat
and book a time on the calendar.

We distribute via Simon & Schuster to bookstores.

Made in the USA
Columbia, SC
18 May 2022